Workbook Ten
Of the Business Essentials
Series

SIMPLY BRILLIANT
CUSTOMER SERVICE

John Millar

ISBN-10:1537058479
ISBN-13:9781537058474

DEDICATION

I dedicate this book to my mother and father, who raised me while self-employed. They taught me to work hard and listen to everyone but to make my own choices as to what is right and what is wrong.. and oh, did I mention work hard?

Anyone who tells you to work smart not hard hasn't ever done it tough and realized that if you work smart AND hard you will achieve more than you can possibly dream.

CONTENTS

PRODUCT DESCRIPTION

Good customer service is the lifeblood of any business. You can offer promotions and slash prices to bring in as many new customers as you want, but unless you can get some of those customers to come back, your business won't be profitable for long.

Good customer service is all about bringing customers back. And about sending them away happy – happy enough to pass positive feedback about your business along to others, who may then try the product or service you offer for themselves and in their turn become repeat customers.

The essence of good customer service is forming a relationship with customers – a relationship that individual customers feel they would like to pursue and share with their friends.

How do you go about forming such a relationship? By remembering the one true secret of good customer service and acting accordingly:

"You will be judged by what you do, not what you say."

Its so easy to give mediocre or good customer service but it's just as easy to give amazing service to your customers and delight them.

You will understand the simple easy steps that you must take to provide consistently brilliant service and how to get your team excited about doing it.

Regards,

John Millar

We've heard it said many times that you know you have the best product and the best company and the best team but if your customer service sucks, then you really have nowhere to go.

Give an example of where you received truly amazing customer service.

....

....

....

....

....

So, what are the essentials of developing outstanding customer service?

1. ....

2. ....

3. ....

4. ....

5. ....

6. ....

7. ....

8. ....

9. ....

10. ....

How are you actually determining why clients leave?

1.
2.
3.
4.
5.

Why are they leaving?

1.
2.
3.
4.
5.
6.
7.
8.

9.

10.

You can't get a second chance at developing a first impression.

> You must develop your active listening skills, make positive language or positive strokes a habit, and also, perfect both your telephone and face to face communication techniques.

> Before we begin, what 10 things do you THINK you need to do to improve in these areas?

1.

2.

3.

4.

5.

6.

7.

8.

9. ....

10. ....

....

Do you understand the difference between aggressive, defensive and assertive behavior over the phone and face to face?

....

....

....

....

....

How do you actually handle complaints?

....

....

....

....

What the profile of your perfect customer?

....

....

....

....

Excellent customer service is customer care that defines and satisfies the customer's experience. Excellent customer care is all about getting the details right.

....

....

....

Take care of the little things, often, big things will take care of themselves.

....
....
....
....

Excellent customer care is all about doing things better than what the customer expects.

....
....
....
....

Remember the ladder of loyalty?

RAVING FAN

ADVOCATE

MEMBER

CUSTOMER

PROSPECT

SUSPECT

Remember what John Calzone said in his book Anytime a customer comes in to contact with any aspect of a business, however remote, it actually forms an impression. And that's what we call a moment of truth.

....
....
....
....
....
....

The story of St. Christopher Wren who re-built St Paul's cathedral after it was destroyed by fire ...

He asked a worker, "what are you doing?"

The worker replied, "Can't you see, I'm laying bricks!"

He asked another worker who said "I'm providing for my family",

and the third worker he asked replied: "I'm building the most beautiful cathedral".

The moral of the story: it's important that everyone on your team identifies with the bigger picture, and how their contribution adds the achievement of the company's goals, mission statement, reason for being. And, full circle, how this impacts them.

How have you developed a vision with our customers to make sure they understand the building blocks of what we're building in our relationship together?

1. ....

2. ....

3. ....

4. ....

5. ....

6. ....

7. ....

8. ....

9. ....

10. ....

....

How have we helped our customers understand that we are human and we do make mistakes and that we are going through a constant period of improvement ourselves?

1.

2.

3.

4.

5.

6.

7.

8.

9.

10.

What do you think you would estimate to be those percentages?

Relocating _____ %

Developing Other Relationships _____ %

Staff Indifference _____ %

Dissatisfaction _____ %

Cost _____ %

Now, let me tell you the real numbers.

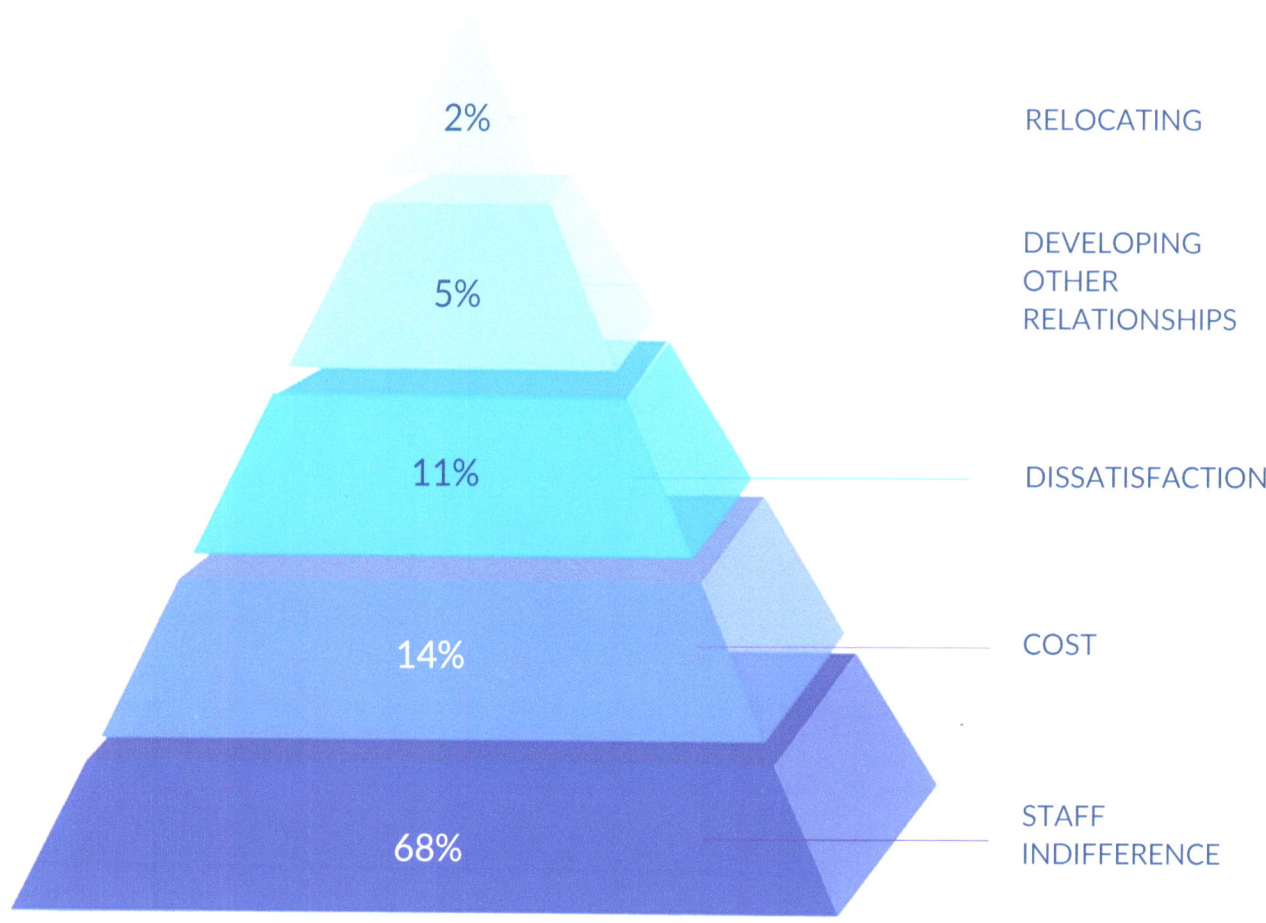

2%   RELOCATING

5%   DEVELOPING OTHER RELATIONSHIPS

11%   DISSATISFACTION

14%   COST

68%   STAFF INDIFFERENCE

A recent study has shown that over 80% of people will stay if you make sure that you take care of their dissatisfaction with your product or service within 24 to 48 hours of the problem occurring. The faster you can fix the problem, the more likelihood you have them staying.

What are the top 10 things you have challenges around that need to be fixed to stop more people leaving?

1.

2.

3.

4.

5.

6.

7.

8.

9.

10.

What do customers really want?

RESPONSIBILITY

TANGIBLES

EMPATHY

ASSURANCE

A recent customer survey asked clients to list what they expect when doing business ...

1. was RELIABILITY – how reliable is your business or service? What checks or test and measure processes do you have in place? Do you have the right systems to ensure your service is reliable and consistent? UNDER PROMISE AND OVER DELIVER.

2. RESPONSIBILITY – moral, ethical, environmental, people within the organization taking responsibility for their roles.

3. ASSURANCE – welcoming "You've come to the right place". We want your business. We value you as a potential customer/client.

4. EMPATHY – Understanding the customer and their needs. Being able to put yourself in their shoes. You need to understand them, not they YOU.

5. TANGIBLES – That's everything they can touch and see; branding, letterheads, website, invoicing, building, vehicles.

What do customers really want?

The average unhappy customer tells 9 to 10 other people about it.

With the proliferation of social media it's easy to air complaints online if you have not looked after someone properly (or perceives you haven't) and now the incident has been exposed immediately to hundreds or thousands or tens of thousands of people...

Remember for every complaint that you receive, there are around 250 people that you dealt with who think that you dealt with them or acted in a way that's rather poor.

Why should you get excited when you do get customer complaints?

Why should you get excited when you do get customer complaints?

....

....

....

....

When was the last time that you undertook a customer survey?

....

....

....

....

If they're done properly, these can provide you with some absolutely outstanding information to let you know who your promoters are, who the detractors are.

....

....

....

....

What are you doing to have a positive impact in customer service?

1. ....

2. ....

3. ....

4. ....

5. ....

6. ....

7. ....

8. ....

9. ....

10. ....

What sort of things would you be looking to achieve with a customer service survey?

1. ....

2. ....

3. ....

4. ....

5. ....

6. ....

7. ....

8. ....

9. ....

10. ....

When was the last time that you actively engaged with your customers to find out what you're doing wrong and what you need to do to be able to step them up so that they can become your active advocates and your raving fans?

....

....

....

....

....

What you can do to exceed your customer's expectations and to really define what you do well and what you'd like to do better.

1. ....

2. ....

3. ....

4. ....

5. ....

6. ....

7. ....

8. ....

9. ....

10. ....

You don't get a second chance to have a first impression.

The three A's of first impressions.

....
....
....
....
....

The first one is your Approach: are you pleasant and yet businesses-like in your greeting?

....
....
....
....

Are you appropriate in the way that you say hello to people?

....
....
....
....

Have you done an Analysis? In other words, do you have the knowledge to give them what they really need from you?

....
....
....
....

Third impression is the A for Action: are you able to articulate and clearly give a course of action to enable you to carry out through a customer satisfaction, the requirements for their needs?

....

....

....

....

....

What are the basic rules of customer care?

....

....

....

....

....

Rule number one; make sure that you acknowledge the customer

....

....

....

....

Rule number two; make sure you put yourself in their shoes.

....

....

....

....

Rule number three; find the need behind the request.

....

....

....

....

80% percent of their decision making around buying from you is going to be made over emotion. The other 20% is logical it's how they justify or create the cause of logic behind it.

Rule number four; exert full responsibility for everything in, on and around your business.

....

....

....

....

Rule number five, make sure that you're involving the customer in the solution.

....

....

....

....

Rule number six is to make sure that you see the issue through until the customer is completely satisfied.

....

....

....

....

What do we do when we actually want to take things from just being basic to being exceptional?

....

....

....

....

First rule is answer when they call.

The second one is, make sure that all times you under promise and over deliver in every single transaction.

The third important basic of the exceptional customer service is to make sure that you keep it personal.

The last point is to make sure that it lives within their mind.

What are the value added propositions that you've added to your service?

1.

2.

3.

4.

5.

6.

7.

8.

9.

10.

What are the extra things that you're going to do a little bit different from your competition?

1. ....

2. ....

3. ....

4. ....

5. ....

6. ....

7. ....

8. ....

9. ....

10. ....

What are the extra things that you're going to do a little bit different from your competition?

....

....

....

....

....

In face to face interactions, less than 7% of your communication is the words that we use. Thirty-eight percent of the communication that we're having when we're face to face is the pitch, pace, time and the timber of our voice because that's what people are hearing. But 55% of all communication is nonverbal communication.

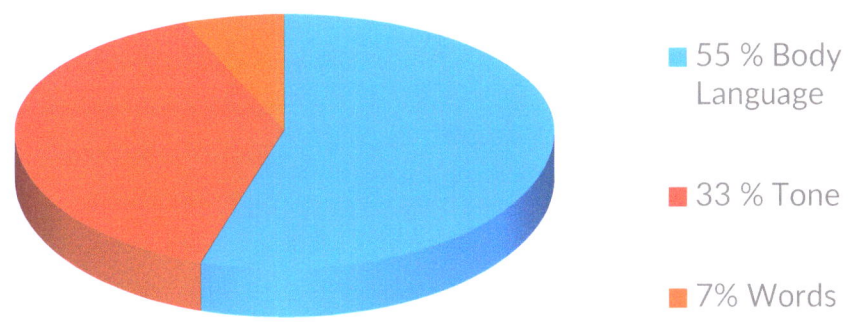

55 % Body Language

33 % Tone

7% Words

Let's look at some positive body language.

The first point is, good eye contact and maintaining good eye contact at least 60% to 70% of the time.

The next thing is make sure that you stand straight. If you're hunched, you could be seen as being concealing something. Make sure that you hold your chin level; it's not too high and it's not too low. If put your chin too high, it looks like you're looking down the nose of somebody in a super silly and condescending manner that really does not make them feel very positive about themselves.

Alternatively, you may not be aware of this, but if you drop your chin lower, you're actually doing two things:

One, you're actually crushing the area of your throat which produces the sound which creates such an important part of your communication; but the other part of it is, that the base instinct of human kind is that this is a very soft, tender and very open area within your body that is very, very vulnerable. So, if you're allowing yourself to become vulnerable, people will actually trust you more. They don't understand why they trust you; it's very much on an instinctive level.

The other thing is, making sure that you're at least an arms-length away from somebody, that you've created that personal space. Have you ever tried communicating with somebody when your personal space is arms-length and they're standing two inches away from your face? It's really hard and people actually step away. Likewise, if you are too far away, it will actually feel like you're maintaining a distance from them, which will not allow them to actually engage with you. But around an arms-length, and that will allow you to move slightly forward or slightly back, depending on the reaction of them to your body language.

Last but not least is making sure that if you do smile, that it's genuine. If you're not genuinely happy to see them or happy to communicate with them, that smile will come across very, very fake and immediately, you've lost the opportunity for positive body language.

Let's have a look at some of the less positive or negative body language areas.

First and foremost is crossed arms. You create a barrier. Now, I see it quite often two people talking, one crosses their arms, they don't even realize that they're doing it. They can actually cross it across their body as well. And it's really just a way of acting as a defensive barrier between the two of us. So, make sure that your arms are uncross and hanging neatly at your side, so that you can actually use it to communicate as well.

The other area is standing with your hands in your pockets. Realistically, if you're trying to communicate effectively in a non-social environment or in a social environment where you're not intimately confident and comfortable with that person, standing with your hands in your pockets are not going to help anybody.

....

....

....

....

....

Slouching, quite the opposite of what we spoke about before which is standing up straight. If you're slouching, it just gives horrible posture and does not allow that person to feel that you are comfortable and confident in talking to them.

....

....

....

....

....

If you're standing with your ankles crossed. It's not an unstable way to stand, but it just also shows a lack of respect in the person that you're speaking to.

....

....

....

....

....

If you're fiddling. Now, a lot of people are fiddlers and jotters. If you're talking to somebody, put that pen down. Don't fiddle with a pen, with your hair, with jewelry, because those fidgets can actually be seen as quite negative body language.

....

....

....

....

If you're frowning — now, it takes far less if to smile than to frown. But often times, our facial features will give away what our mouth is not saying. So, make sure that we maintain a positive demeanor.

The next point is actually NOT having a poker face. Make sure that your face is animated, that it's actually expressing the joy and the gratitude that you have in communicating and dealing with the people that you are talking to.

Another one is yawning. the reality is, when you yawn, it shows people, whether it's true or not, that you're disinterested in what they have to say.

The other thing is looking at a clock or watch. Set an alarm if you must. If I've got a meeting with somebody and we've got 30 minutes in a meeting, I will set a vibrate alarm or a soft alarm to remind me that I have five minutes left in that meeting, but don't constantly look at your clock or your watch. Because then, all you're doing is just saying, well, I really can't wait for our interaction to be finished.

What are 10 things that you can actually do to improve your positive body language?

1.

2.

3.

4.

5.

6.

7.

8.

9.

10.

Not everything we do is communicating face to face. Quite a lot of it is actually over the phone.

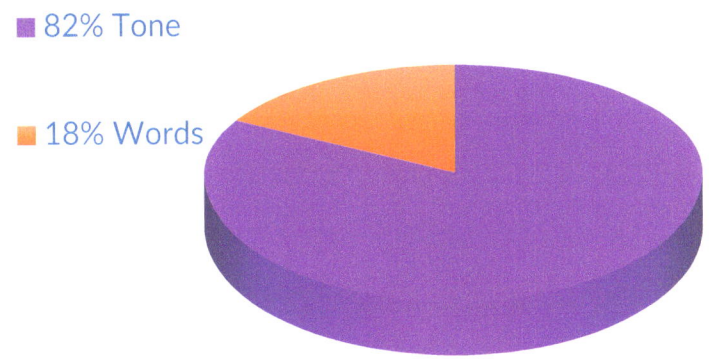

When we're communicating over the phone, we only have two mediums to be able to work on: And one is, the words that we use and the second one is how we actually say it — — the pitch, pace, timber and time, et cetera, of your voice.

....
....
....
....

18% of communication when talking on the phone is actually the words that you use.

....
....
....
....

Far more attention is being taken up into the words that you use. So, make sure that if you say something, you mean what you say. There's was an absolutely fantastic philosopher and leader of the human potential movement over the last 50 years his name is Buckminster Fuller. He took a vow of silence for two years. because he said something that was taken the wrong way by somebody else and it had some serious consequences. He made sure after he started speaking again that whenever he communicated, he would use words that with the most powerful possible so there would be no misunderstanding.

The other 82% when we're communicating over the phone is that pitch, pace, time and the way that we express things.

Try this, when you answer the phone stand up to make sure that your diaphragm is released and that you can actually speak and breathe naturally. You can hear the difference in somebody's voice to when they're sitting, to when they're standing.

A very, very important part of that communication process over the phone is making sure that we listen and understand what actually interferes with our capacity to listen.

When we actually have something that interferes with our listening, it creates a gap between hearing and active listening.

We need to foster ways to engender greater techniques for active listening.

Now, what do I mean by active listening?

Passive listening, I'm sitting back waiting for you to say something without any real thought about what you said, what you are saying and what you may be saying. Active listening takes those other three aspects right into control.

What are the obstacles for listening?

One, is that physical distractions or the background noise

Another one is what we call emotional deafness. So in other words, I hear what you're saying but I don't really hear what you're saying. You're not listening to the way that they're saying it, what their pitch, tone and pace might be. And you're not actually attuned to where they're coming from.

The next obstacle is usually boredom or disinterest. I have heard the same rubbish time and time again, or I'm sick of my job. So, if you appear bored or disinterested, that's a massive obstacle for listening. You can't do that if you're actively listening and actively engaged.

A massive obstacle to listening— is a lack of concentration. So often, when I've worked with clients with large call centers or with small teams that can't rotate their duties around, we find that they've been stuck in the rut of doing the same thing. You cannot maintain concentration. I advise getting up and doing things regularly which might just be simply standing up to stretch your legs and sit back down again. These small breaks of state will allow you to maintain a high level of concentration and allow the opportunity to remain fully engaged.

Active listening can mean taking notes. If you're taking notes, then you're hearing it and you give yourself an opportunity to be able to repeat back to them what they've said.

Another way to show active listening is nodding, smiling or other physical reactions like facial expressions, that actually show that you're intend, eye contact, making sure that you're leaning forward, area you really interested and are you showing that in a physical way.

Make sure that you have an upright and attentive posture. If you're sitting there with your arms crossed and legs crossed and half twisted away from somebody, that might look a little gangster, but the reality is it's not showing that you're being truly attentive to the person that you're dealing with.

Make sure that we match and mirror the other person's urgency.

Listen for verbal skills. Which is uhm, really, yeah, nah. Those verbal listening skills. The reason why people say uhm, is because their brain hasn't caught up with their mouths. Or it has become such an ingrained habit that they had to make sure that they address those issues before they go any further.

....

....

....

....

Look for when people actually ask further probing questions. Questions to get clarity and a better understanding about what's actually being said.

....

....

....

....

....

....

....

Look at what you can do to make sure that you are actively listening to people and the signs that you're actually being disinterested.

1. ....

2. ....

3. ....

4. ....

5. ....

6. ....

7.

8.

9.

10.

An important part of communicating with people is actually being able to phrase things and put them in a way that's a little more positive manner.

> **If I was to say these three different things, what are the better ways that we can actually say it?**

First, look, it's not going to be possible to send this to you for at least three days. Would it not have been better to communicate with somebody and say, look, certainly I can organize it for you, and, you know, I'll have it to you within four days, on or before four days.

> **We've said the same things but we've said it in a way that's rephrased in a far more palatable manner.**

The second example is, look, I don't know about anything about this. But Linda, in accounts, she might be able to help.

Now, doesn't that feel like somebody's duck shoving or avoiding the issue rather than taking responsibility? Why wouldn't we want to say something like this, "Linda on accounts can help you with that. I'll put you through. And if I can help you in any way, please let me know." So, Linda on accounts can help you with this, I'll put you through. But if you still need my help, please let me know. What a much nicer way to be able to say the same thing and doesn't sound like we're avoiding the issue at all.

Last but not least, "Look, if you don't pay your bill in full, you're going to lose your credit with us." How much more of a positive result would you get with somebody if you said, "Look, Frank, to maintain your good credit rating with us, we'd really appreciate it if you could settle your account with us in full by Wednesday or the following Friday where it's better for you." So, you're asking the same thing. You're telling them that it's important but you're approaching the situation in a way that works.

> Find a way to respond to questions in the vernacular, in the phrases, in the words that you use that you feel most comfortable with.

You must be able to understand the words that you use so that you can use the best possible words most appropriately at the right time.

We need to have language which is solid and something that cannot be misunderstood.

....

....

....

....

We need to avoid jargon and acronyms. Now, what do I mean by jargon and acronyms? Jargon re words which you commonly use in your industry that most of us normal people wouldn't have a clue what you've just said. And an acronym is a shortening or an abbreviation of something which, again, is common knowledge to you but to rest of us is really not well known.

....

....

....

....

Use personal, positive and persuasive words

According to surveys, these are the most persuasive words we can HEAR.

Why not write a sentence about your service, using as many of these words as you can …

For example:

"our new management development and training program is easy to follow and is certain to provide you with proven results that are guaranteed to save you time and money; it's free for our one on one clients and I'm extremely confident you're going to love the experience".

....
....
....
....

Live and die by the following rules

First and foremost, speak in the tone that gives an impression of honesty and respect.

....
....
....
....
....

Second speak clearly, articulate well.

....
....
....

Modulate your voice so that it's neither too loud or too soft.

....
....
....

Project energy and enthusiasm through the way that we use our voice.

Make sure the rhythm is right. Make sure that your pace is neither too fast nor too slow.

Remember: People who speak slower are not stupid, but they may process information slower and in a more considerate manner. People who speak a lot quicker may in fact be able to process that information or their enthusiasm or ebullient nature just merely means that they race ahead of themselves.

When we're talking over the phone, we've actually got three stages within that call.

The first stage is the professional answer. Have you got a scripted way that you answer the phone? Do you make sure that you answer the phone in a way that engenders trust, enthusiasm and excitement that you're very glad that the phone rang? Or are you answering, oh, yeah, what do you want?

The second stage is make sure that you get the information or able to impart the information correctly and efficiently. Are you able to take control of the conversation without seeming like you've taken control? Have you use open-ended questions?

Make sure that you record and write down and repeat, or at least make listening noises. How often have you been speaking to someone that's being completely silent on the other end? You don't know that they've been actively listening to you, but they haven't responded with those answers of uh-huh, yup, OK, I got it, I understand, oh, that's great.

The third and really important stage in any call is making sure that we get or give any extra information before wrapping the call up. There's nothing worse than concluding a conversation with some and said, well, hang on a second, I didn't really get a chance to ask them that question or, gee, I wish I have had told them this that way they've got something more to consider. So, the best way to do that is to offer them help. So, look, if you need me further help, just give me a buzz.

Make sure that you have volunteered what is actually useful information. So, what I'd like you to do now is to actually take a few minutes and think about what you can actually do to cover those areas within every call and making sure that you're communicating with each other as effectively as possible.

What are some of the areas of where can be seen as being aggressive towards a customer?

You can be patronizing towards a customer.

The old attitude "the customer is always right" is rubbish. You know it, I know it and the customer knows it as well. They're not always right. But we don't win anything if all we're doing is we're trying to take an aggressive stance towards making the customer feel like they're to blame.

Avoid the opportunity in any aggressive behavior that gets the customer feeling like they're actually inferior to you.

Never ever, ever let them feel that they're nuisance because that's worse than perceived apathy.

Ignoring the customer by not returning calls or emails etc particularly when the customer needs help won't help anyone.

Pretending to be a little bit smart is actually stupid.

When dealing with behavior, what we're seeing is just the tip of the iceberg; at least 70 or 80% of the reason behind the behavior is beneath the surface – we can't see it. So we tend to judge the person and the circumstance based on the behavior we can see – particularly when we use our EMOTIONAL brain, rather than our THINKING brain.

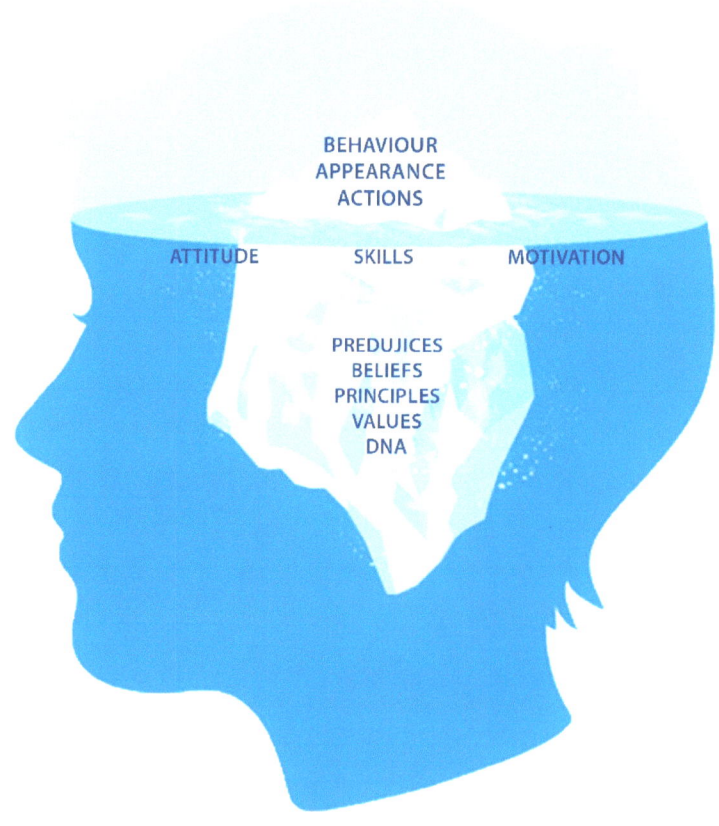

If we look at your brain, we break it down into the emotional brain. You've got one part of your brain which is very immediate, instinctive, impulsive and quite irrational. And in that part of our brain we react in either an aggressive or a submissive manner. And that's not particularly helpful. It's good to have an emotional brain and to have those areas, but making sure that we control the outcome from that emotional brain. On the other side, we look at our thinking brain. And that's our constructive, problem solving, controlled and rational part of our brain. It's where we move from we-centered. When under an emotional brain, we use a little bit of that "it's all about me," it's I-centered. The thinking is all about we-centered. It's what allows us to active and show assertive behavior that we're in control of a situation and that we can guard it. You notice I didn't said the words "we can guard it" because it's all about us.

When you're actually being assertive, we need to use I-statements like I think and I feel. Make sure that your voice is steady and firm, and try not to hesitate because hesitation can be seen as a lack of assertiveness. Make sure that you speak in well-modulated voice, neither too loud nor too soft. Too loud, because you're scared and therefore have to try and get louder.

> **Do you ever have those arguments or a heated discussion with someone who seems to think that the louder they get and the faster they speak, the more right they suddenly become?**

Likewise, if you're talking to somebody and they're talking a little bit too soft, that can show timidity and reserve in what they're actually doing. Don't be tense.

When you're being assertive, give advice in a form of a question of; have you considered, have you thought about, what about this? This way you are asking them in a way that you're telling them what needs to be done.

....

....

Make sure at all times that your posture is erect, that you sit upright and that your head and chin are held up.

....

....

....

....

....

When you're actually asking questions, seek a joint solution. So, how can we achieve this? Is there something more that we can work on together?

....

....

....

....

> **Write down a series of questions and things that you need to do to be more assertive when the situations is far more appropriate.**

1. ....
2. ....
3. ....
4. ....
5. ....
6. ....
7. ....
8. ....
9. ....
10. ....

What's actually going to happen in regards to my submissive behavior?

....
....
....
....

What am I doing around my aggressive behavior?

....
....
....
....

What's that doing to create the outcome that I want to achieve?

....
....
....
....

Did you identify the difference between being assertive and being aggressive and how you can actually go about applying that every day in what you're doing?

....
....
....
....

Being assertive is not necessarily a bad thing.

Let's have a look at some of the benefits of actually showing assertive behavior, one that actually helps us to create a good impression.

....
....
....
....

It makes us more confident.

www.moreprofitlesstime.com | www.ceo-ondemand.com   45

It actually puts you into control of the situation.

It enables you to build a good working relationship and it makes you feel good about the way that you behave.

Are you assertive enough that people know that they can communicate with you clearly, confidently and professionally with a high level of honesty and integrity?

Remember: assertive behavior is not necessarily aggressive behavior. Assertive behavior is all about treating people with respect, not generating fear.

There are six stages in actually handling complaints within our business.

Stage number one you need to listen actively. You need to make sure that you listen to the facts without assuming anything first, making sure that you're open and aware.

Secondly is to empathize. Now, I didn't say agree, but coming quickly with empathy of "I understand why you feel annoyed." You're not necessarily agreeing with them, you're not necessarily giving that issue or that complaint credence or credibility, but you're empathizing with them. You're not empathizing with the problem; you're empathizing with the way that they're feeling about the problem.

The third part of the six stages is to probe. Make sure that you ask quality questions that allow them to clarify the exact nature of the problem. You need to establish all of the facts. If you don't do that, then how do you know that you're able to handle them effectively?

The fourth stage is to solve the problem. Present them with alternatives and agree on a mutually beneficial solution that you both feel as acceptable. If the matter is unresolved, it will only lead to further complaints. So, make sure that we resolve it one way or the other as quickly as possible.

The fifth is to take personal responsibility whether its' your fault or not, we're not talking about blaming or justifying or anything a little nasty like that. We're talking about apologizing and taking responsibility on behalf of your organization. Look, I'm really that that occurred. I'm so glad that you raised it and I'm glad that we're able to fix that together. At no stage have I said it was my fault. But what I've done is I've taken responsibility and apologize in a meaningful and sincere way.

Last but not least in the six steps is to make sure that you're absolutely certain the undertaking is carried out. It's very frustrating when somebody promises something will be done to handle a complaint, you agree on a solution, but they haven't actually followed it through to make sure that that action was taken care of. How great is that if you're actually able to overcome it, and then somebody else gets back to you and says, "Mrs. Jones, I was just contacting you because you had this issue. Now, I know that we've resolved it, but I just wanted to be sure that you are absolutely happy and delighted with our service. And is there anything more that we can do?" So, follow up, follow up, follow up, follow up.

> You can't change the mistake that's caused the complaint. You may have been able to fix the system to ensure that that never occurs again, but what you need to do is follow this through to its ultimate conclusions.

So that people actually in my organizations understand things easily I actually have boundaries of blue rules and red rules.

> Blue rules are the sorts of rules that can't harm the organization in any way.

The other rules are red rules. Now, why do I have it as a red rule? Because red is a warning. Red is distinctive and it's something that we know and are raised with — that's a color that needs special attention. These are rules that if broken could be detrimental to the organization or the people within it.

When we're breaking a blue rule, we need to actually show empathy and probe the reasons and understand why. We need to make sure that we say something along the lines. Well, normally, I can't do that because, remember, it is rule, it's a blue rule but it's still the rule. Normally, I can't do that because — but I'll be able to help you in this state. So, when you explain that you can help, you know, I can make a special exception just for you. It's special and it's an exception.

The customer understands the rules of the game that this is a rule but we're being flexible in that regard. And finally, part of that breaking the blue rule is to remind them that the rules are there to adjust to help them. But they need to comply in the future.

How many blue rules are actually inside your business and what can you do to make sure you identify them and help people understand it?

1.

2.

3.

4.

5.

6.

7.

8.

9.

10.

Make sure that you take the opportunity to have all of your custom service standards, expectations and deliverables really clear and visible. Make sure that your staff, your clients, the supplies, everybody can see it.

When you get this right — you will stand out in a sea of mediocrity.

Additional Information

John Millar
Managing Director
More Profit Less Time Pty Ltd
Profit facilitator, Author, Business and Executive Coach, Trainer, Professional Speaker
Certified Business Coach, Certified NLP Practitioner, Certified Guerrilla Marketing Practitioner
Diploma of Management, Diploma of Human Resources Management, Cert IV TAE

How to Use Scripts to Ensure Consistency in Customer Service

a) Is your first reaction like that of my clients–scripting doesn't work, scripting is too artificial, scripting doesn't take into account different personalities? I've heard just about every excuse as to why scripts won't work; but, as I wean my clients onto the idea and they see their bottom line increasing, converts are made. Here's how to get started.

b) The four main areas to consider when writing a script are:

- Target Market – be very clear who you're trying to reach.
- Process – some of the more expensive products and services may require several steps before a sale is made.
- Urgency – you must give people a reason to act now.
- 'You' Focus – your script needs to be focused towards the customer.

c) Within the script itself you then need to look at:
- Greeting – Get this right as it will set the tone for what follows.
- Outline the reason for your call/visit and get permission to continue – e.g. "Would it be OK if I outlined the reason for my call today?" This step applies when you're the one making the first contact.
- Ask open-ended questions – you must ask questions that can't be answered by yes or no.

d) Get agreement–you need to get feedback from the customer. Ask rhetorical questions that will get them to say yes–e.g. "So it sounds like you'd benefit from A, B and C, that's pretty good, isn't it?"

e) Deal with objections – this is part of the process! Get the customer to elaborate, acknowledge that what they're saying is true for them at the time and then come up with your standard replies to known objections.

Customer Service PHONE Performance Standards

f) Close and take the next step – Would you like to pay by check or credit card?"

g) Use transition phrases/temperature checking phrases like, "How does this fit with what you had in mind?," "So from what I understand, you want A, B and C. Is there anything else?"

You will end up with a script that is really effective as a sales tool. More importantly, your entire team will have a framework to follow, which means your customers will be treated in a like-minded fashion regardless of who speaks to them. This, in turn, enhances the perception of excellent customer service. An added bonus, if you needed another one, is that any new team member will be productive much more quickly. Go make it happen!

How poorly do all of our mobile phone message banks and answering skills stack up?

Performance Standard #1

SMILE....until you feel it, BEFORE you pick up the phone

Performance Standard #2

Answer every call AFTER the 2nd ring but BEFORE the third ring

Performance Standard #3

Greet people by saying....

"Good morning/afternoon, thanks for calling <Buz. Name>. This is...<your name>".

Performance Standard #4

Don't screen and always ask permission to put on someone on hold.
Never say a person is 'in a meeting', they are always 'with someone'

Performance Standard #5

Listen attentively and give out positive strokes ("Yes", "I see", "I understand" etc)

Performance Standard #6

Ask Questions irrespective....
- The Magic Question is; "Thanks for your call, just so that I can help you best, would it be OK if I asked you a couple of questions"

Performance Standard #7

Give out little pieces of information and talk in the caller's language

Performance Standard #8

Check the caller's Temperature and ask a detail question
- Temperature: "How does that fit with what you had in mind…?
- Detail question: "How would you like to pay for that", "When would you like that delivered" etc.

Performance Standard #9

Confirm the order and confirm their Phone Number
 - Getting Information: "It's….." (and stay silent!)

Performance Standard #10

Thank your caller

Performance Standard #11

Make sure you hang up LAST, and leave your caller on a HIGH.

What image are you portraying to everyone that does business with you???

Top 10 Ways to Keep Your Customers Happy

The old adage, "it costs five times more to attract a new customer as it does keeping an old one," still holds true today. This simple economics lesson should encourage you to do what you can to keep your customers happy and coming back for return business. But how can you improve customer satisfaction and retain customers? Here are 10 easy tips you can implement to keeping your customers happy and loyal.

1. Acknowledge customers

Whether by answering a phone call right away, or with eye contact and a simple "I'll be right with you," acknowledging your customers immediately will go a long way in improving customer satisfaction.

2. Know your customers

Literally. Find out their names and greet them by name whenever possible. Get birthday information and send them a special offer or treat on their birthday. This can help improve customer satisfaction by knowing you care about them as individuals.

3. Reward customer loyalty

One strategy to keeping customers happy is to reward them for loyalty. Many businesses have a "buy 5 – get 1 free" card or something similar. Though this is good, you can also reward customers unexpectedly. After a few visits with a return customer, give them a complimentary drink, an added service, or even a gift card.

4. Go the extra mile

Loyal customers like to know you will go the extra mile. If there is a problem, solve the problem and give the customer something extra to let them know they are important to you.

5. Follow up

Customers do not like to follow up for updated information. If you tell a customer you are looking into an issue, be sure to follow up on a regular basis with the status. A phone call or email can make the difference in a happy customer and a disgruntled one.

6. Give special offers to current customers

Use your customer contacts to offer a "members only" type of promotion to current customers. This improves customer satisfaction by making them feel valued and part of an "inside" group.

7. Keep in touch

Try to acquire customer contact information. Then send regular updates via mail or email. A quarterly newsletter is a good way of keeping customers informed of news and simply reminding them of your business name.

8. Differentiate from the competition

Whether you design a creative interior to your retail store or simply provide more value through exceptional customer service, you must keep customers happy by setting yourself apart from your competition.

9. Ask customers for their opinions

What do your customers want? It never hurts to ask customers about their experience and what improvements they would like. This can provide valuable information on how you can improve products and your service delivery.

10. Give samples

Do you have a new product? Current customers can be a good source of market research. Give free samples to existing customers and ask their valued opinion. Keeping your existing customers happy and loyal is the best way to maintain your company's revenues.

In addition, your happy customers will naturally spread the word about your business, which kills two birds with one stone for your long-term growth.

When Times are Tough, Service Matters

Today, we seem to be bombarded constantly with news of the difficulties faced by business. A stock market struggling to recover from an almost unprecedented bear run, falling industrial investment, more bureaucracy, credit worries, high street spending in decline – are we in recession, or is it merely a 'severe downturn'?

Is it **all** bad news? Certainly not. Is there anything a businessperson can do to overcome these pressures? Absolutely...but success in these challenging times is never easy. As always, it demands commitment, hard work and **an obsession with customer service**.

In difficult economic times, many businesses focus on cutting costs – an understandable and generally prudent thing to do. But some try to cut costs by cutting corners on customer service. This is exactly the **wrong** thing to do. Right now, service matters more than ever.

Here's why:

- When people buy during an economic downturn they are extremely conscious of the "hard earned" money that they spend. Customers want **more** attention, appreciation and recognition for their purchases, not less.

- Customers want to be sure they get maximum value for the money they choose to spend. They want assistance, education, training, installation, modifications and support. The basic product may remain the same, **but they want more service.**

- Customers want stronger guarantees that their purchase was "the right thing to do". In good times, a single bad purchase may be quickly overlooked or forgotten, but in tough times, **every** expenditure is scrutinized. Provide the assurance your customers seek with generous service guarantees, regular follow-up and speedy follow-through on any queries or complaints.

- In tough times, people spend less time travelling, wining and dining, and more time carefully shopping for each and every purchase. Giving good service enhances the customer's shopping experience, and boosts **your** own business' image.

- When times are good, people make decisions quickly and sometimes don't notice your efforts. In tighter times, people move more cautiously, and notice every extra effort that you make.

- When money is tight, many people experience a sense of lower self-esteem. When they get good service from your business it boosts their self-image. And when they feel good about themselves, they feel good about you. And when they feel good about you, they buy.

- In tough times, people talk more with each other about saving money and getting good value. "Positive word of mouth" is a powerful force at any time. In difficult times, even more ears will be listening. Be sure the words spoken about your business are good ones.

So giving great service in tough times makes good business sense. But how do you actually achieve it? Here are eight proven principles you can use:

1. Understand how your customers' expectations are rising and changing over time. What was good enough last year may not be good enough now. Use customer surveys, interviews and focus groups to really understand what your customers want, what they value, and think about what they are getting, (or not getting) from your business.

2. Use quality service to differentiate your business from your competition. Your products must be reliable and up to date ... but your competitors' are likely to be, too. Your delivery systems must be fast and user-friendly, but so are your competitors'! Make a real difference by providing personalized, responsive and "extra-mile service" that stands out in a unique way which customers will appreciate and remember.

3. Set and achieve high service standards. Go beyond basic and expected levels of service to provide your customers with desired and even surprising interactions. Determine the "norm" for service in your industry, and then find a way to go beyond it. Give more choice than "usual", be more flexible than "normal", be "faster" than the average and extend a "better" warranty than all the others.
Your customers will notice your higher standards. But eventually even the highest standards can be copied by your competitors. So don't slow down. Keep on improving.

4. Learn to manage your customer's expectations. You can't always give customers everything their hearts desire. Sometimes you need to bring their expectations into line with what you know you can deliver. The best way to do this is by first building a reputation for making and keeping clear promises. Once you have established a base of trust and good reputation, you only need to ask your customers for their patience in the rare circumstances when you cannot meet their first requests. Nine times out of 10 they will extend the understanding and the leeway that you need. The second way to manage customer's expectations (indeed, to exceed them) is with the tactic called "Under Promise and Over Deliver". It works like this: your customer wants something done fast. You know it will take one hour to complete. Don't tell your customer. Let them know you will rush the project...but then promise 90 minutes. Then, when you are done in just an hour (as you knew you would be all along), your customer will be delighted that you actually finished the job "so quickly".

5. Bounce back with effective service recovery. Sometimes things do go wrong. When it happens to your customers, do everything you can to make things right again, as soon as possible. Fix the problem. Show sincere concern for any discomfort, frustration or inconvenience. Then "do a little bit more" by giving your customers something positive to remember–a token of goodwill, a small gift of appreciation, a discount on future orders, or an upgrade to a higher class of product.

This is not the time to lay blame for what went wrong, or to calculate the costs of repair. Restoring customer goodwill is worth the price in future orders and new business.

6. Appreciate your complaining customers. Customers with complaints can be your best allies in building and improving your business. They point out where your system is faulty, and where procedures are weak or problematic. They show you where your products are below expectations or your service doesn't measure up. They point out areas where your competitors are getting ahead, or where your team is falling behind. These are the same insights and conclusions that people pay consultants to provide...but a "complainer" gives them to you free.

And remember, for every one person who complains, there are many more that won't even bother to tell you. The others just take their business elsewhere. At least the complainer gives you a chance to reply and set things right.

7. Take personal responsibility. In many organizations, people are quick to blame others for problems or difficulties at work: managers blame staff, staff blame managers, engineering blames sales, sales blames marketing and everyone blames finance. This doesn't help. In fact, with all the finger-pointing going on, it tends to make things worse.

Blaming yourself doesn't work either. No matter how many mistakes you may have made, tomorrow is another chance to do better. You need high self-esteem to give good service. Feeling "ashamed" doesn't help.

It doesn't make sense to blame the computers, the system or the budget, either. This kind of justification only prolongs the pain before the necessary changes take place.

The most reliable way to bring about constructive change in your organization is to take personal responsibility and help make good things happen. Make recommendations, propose new ideas, give your suggestions, volunteer to help out with problem-solving teams and projects. .

See the world from your customers' point of view. We often get so caught up in our own world that we lose sight of what our customers actually experience

8. Make time to stand on the other side of the counter, or listen on the other end of the phone. Be a "mystery shopper" at your own place of business. Or be a customer for your competition. What you notice is what your customers experience every day!

Why Customers Stop Buying?

Finally, remember that service is the currency that keeps our economy moving. "I serve you in one business, you serve me in another." When either of us improves, the economy gets a little better. When both of us improve, people are sure to take notice. When everyone improves, the whole economy grows stronger and there is no longer any reason for the depressing headlines to which we've become so accustomed. So, let's all start looking after our customers and let the economy look after itself. Perhaps not a solution Mr. Greenspan would endorse – but, then, what has he ever really known about the nuts and bolts of being in business?

And that's worth thinking about...

There are only 5 reasons...
There are five–and only five–reasons why people STOP BUYING.

- **4%** are gone. They move, get promoted, transferred, divorced, die or whatever. They are simply no longer in a position to make a buying decision.
- **5%** change suppliers on the recommendation of a friend or business associate. Stay in touch with them, you may get them back–sometimes quickly.
- **9%** change because of a true competitive advantage; an honest benefit offered over your product or service, and usually this means price.
- **14%** change because they are unhappy with your service or product. (You're better off turning a customer away, than selling them something that's not right for them. This way you build trust and leave the door open to come back when you feel you have something that fills their needs. Selling something that's totally wrong for the customer can close the door on you forever.)
- **68% of People stop buying from you because of a perceived lack of caring service expressed by your company!**

Creating a Powerful Guarantee and USP for better customer service

That's 68% of customers you never had to lose. They did not think that you cared if they returned and bought off you or not. You had not kept in touch with them or shown them in any way that you valued them as a client or appreciated their business with you.
(By the way, resolving a customer complaint quickly and efficiently will save 95% of the customers who complain. Just listening to a customer's complaint will salvage more than 50% of them!)

Sources: From U.S. government study "Why Customers Stop Buying." Comments by Warren Greshes and Bob Mellon

Again, the easiest way to get started here is to answer a few questions, just to get you thinking. To come up with a powerful guarantee, you need to know what your customers want you to guarantee, and what you actually can promise.

The idea is to match your abilities with your customers' wants. Often, it's a good idea to over promise. You probably underrate your product or service anyway. If you think it's good, why not promise that it will be great–it'll make you pick up your act, and probably be more in line with your current customers' perceptions anyway.

Here are the questions...

What is your current guarantee?

....

....

....

....

What are 3 problems or frustrations buying your product/service solves?

1. ....

2. ....

3. ....

What frustrations do customers experience when trying to find your product or service?

....

....

....

....

What frustrations do customers experience when they go to buy your product or service?

....

....

....

....

What are the 3 major benefits of buying your product or service?

1. ....

2. ....

3. ....

What frustrations do customers experience when using your product or service?

....

....

....

....

What frustrations do customers experience after they've bought your product or service (e.g.– lack of after-sales service)?

....

....

....

....

If you were a customer, why would you dislike buying from you?

....

....

....

....

....

....

_____

_____

_____

_____

_____

_____

_____

_____

_____

Describe the sort of potential customers who love buying from you ... and why?

_____

_____

_____

If you could easily overcome any 2 of your customers frustrations what would they be and how would you overcome them?

1. _____

2. _____

What 6 things that will relieve your customer's frustrations that you can guarantee, and deliver 100% of the time right now?

1. _____

2. _____

3. _____

4. _____

5.

6.

What 3 additional things will you be able to fully guarantee within the next 3 months?

1.

2.

3.

List 3 things that you can NOT confidently guarantee today, that you would love to be able to guarantee tomorrow …

1.

2.

3.

What is the ONE thing that, if you could guarantee it, would make you the market leader? (For example, a news agency that guarantees to sell you a winning lottery ticket every time). Is there any way in the world, within the realms of human possibility, that you could offer this; even it backfired some of the time?

Habits of going the extra mile

Napoleon Hill spent most of his life studying the most successful entrepreneurs in American history. He analyzed men like Ford, Edison and Carnegie at length. He concluded that success followed predictable and distinct patterns of behavior. He suggested that all men and women have similar options open to them. He argued that great success and achievement were available to any and all who would choose to follow certain requirements which he spelled out in his many books.

Mr. Hill was the architect of the philosophy of success. He was a pioneer and an original thinker. Many books and articles have copied his ideas, but he remains the master. Of all the great human accomplishments in the 20th century, the judgment of history will inevitably rank the commentaries of Napoleon Hill among them.

The following outlines some of Napoleon Hill's greatest success philosophies. Please read this with the intent of employing key principles into your life, and impart this wisdom directly to those around you...

***

An important principle of success in all walks of life and in all occupations is a willingness to Go the Extra Mile; the rendering of more and better service than that for which one is paid, and giving it in a positive mental attitude. Search wherever you will for a single sound argument against this principle, and you will not find it, nor will you find a single instance of enduring success which was not attained in part by its application.

Many may disregard the principle if he chooses, but he cannot do so and at the same time enjoy the fruits of enduring success.

The advantages of the habit of going the extra mile are definite and understandable. Let me examine some of them:

The habit brings the individual to the favorable attention of those who can and will provide opportunities for self-advancement.

It tends to make one indispensable, in many different human relationships and it therefore enables him to command more than average compensation for personal services.

It leads to mental growth and to physical skill and perfection in many forms of endeavor; thereby adding to one's earning capacity.

It enables one to profit by the law of contrast, since the majority of people do not practice the habit.

It leads to the development of a positive, pleasing mental attitude, which is essential for enduring success.

It tends to develop a keen, alert imagination because it is a habit which inspires one continuously to seek new and better ways of rendering service.

It develops the important quality of personal initiative.

It develops the self-reliance and courage.

It serves to build the confidence of others in one's integrity.

It aids the mastery of the destructive habit of procrastination.

It develops definiteness of purpose, insuring one against the common habit of aimlessness.

There is still another and a great reason for following the habit of going the extra mile. It gives one the only logical reason for asking for increased compensation. If a man performs no more service that that for which he is being paid, then obviously he is receiving all the pay to which he is entitled. He must render as much service as that for which he is being paid, in order to maintain his source of income, regardless of how he earns.

But he has the privilege always of rendering a surplus of service as a means of accumulating a reserve credit of goodwill, and to provide a just reason for demanding more pay, a better position, or both.

Any practice of philosophy which deprives a man of the privilege of going the extra mile is unsound and doomed to failure, for it is obvious that this principle is the stepping-stone of major importance by which an individual may receive compensation for extraordinary skill, experience and education; and it is the one principle which provides the way of self-determination, regardless of what occupation, profession or calling the individual may be engaged in.

In our societies, anyone may earn a living without the habit of going the extra mile. Any many do just that, but the economic security and luxuries available are available only to the individual who makes this principle a part of his philosophy of life and lives by it as a matter of daily habit.

Every known rule of logic and common sense forces one to accept this as true. And even a cursory analysis of men in the higher brackets of success will prove that it is true.

It is a well-known fact that Andrew Carnegie developed more successful leaders of industry than has any other great American industrialist. Most of them came up from the ranks of ordinary day laborers and many of them accumulated personal fortunes of vast amounts, more than they could acquire without the guidance of Mr. Carnegie.

The first test that Mr. Carnegie applied to any worker whom he desired to promote was that of determining to what extent the worker was willing to go the extra mile.

It was this test that led to the discovery of Charles M. Schwab. When Mr. Schwab first came to Mr. Carnegie's attention he was working as a day laborer in one of the steel master's plants.

Close observation revealed that Mr. Schwab always performed more and better service that that for which he was paid. Moreover, he performed it in a pleasing mental attitude which made him popular among his fellow workers.

Truly it pays to go the extra mile, for every time an individual does so he places someone else under obligation to him.

No one is forced to develop the habit of going the extra mile and seldom is anyone ever requested to render more service than that for which he is paid. Therefore, if the habit is followed it must be adopted on one's own initiative.

keeper and, at the same time, rewards him for so doing.

It was this very asset which enabled Charles M. Schwab to climb, step by step, from the lowly beginning as a day laborer to the highest position his employee had to offer and it was this asset as well which brought Mr. Schwab a bonus of more than ten times the amount of his salary.

No one ever does anything voluntarily without a motive. Let us see if we can reveal a sound motive that will justify the habit of going the extra mile by observing a few who have been inspired by it.

Many years ago an elderly lady was strolling through a Pittsburgh department store. She passed counter after counter without anyone paying any attention to her. All of the clerks had spotted her as an idle "looker" who had no intention of buying. They made it a point of looking in another direction when she stopped at their counters.

What a costly business this neglect turned out to be!

Finally the lady came to a counter that was attended by a young clerk who bowed politely and asked if he might serve her.

"No," she replied, "I am just killing time, waiting for the rain to stop so I can go home".

"Very well, Madam," the young man smiled, "may I bring out a chair for you?" And he brought it without waiting for an answer. After the rain slacked, the young man took the lady by the arm, escorted her to the street and bade her good-bye. As she left she asked him for his card.

Several months later, the owner of the store received a letter, asking that this young man be sent to Scotland to take an order for the furnishings of a home. The owner of the store wrote back that he was sorry, but the young man did not work in the house furnishings department. However, he explained that he would be glad to send an "experienced man" to do his job.

Back came a reply that no one would do except this particular young man. The letters were signed by Andrew Carnegie, and the "house" he wanted furnished was Skibo Castle in Scotland. The elderly lady was Mr. Carnegie's mother. The young man was sent to Scotland. He received an order for several hundred thousand dollars' worth of household furnishings. He later became the owner of half interest in the store.

Truly it pays to go the extra mile.

There is something about this habit of doing more than one is compensated for which works on one's behalf even while he sleeps. Once it begins to work, it piles up riches so fast that it seems like queer magic. Like Aladdin's Lamp, it draws to one's aid an army of genies which come laden with bags of gold.

Here is the appropriate place to remind you of an important thing about the habit of doing more than one is paid for. It is the strange influence which it has on the person who does it. The greatest benefit from this habit does not come to those to whom the service is rendered. It comes to the one who renders the service, in the form of a changed "mental attitude", which gives him more influence with other people, more self-reliance, greater initiative, more enthusiasm, more vision and definitive purpose. All of these are qualities of successful achievement.

"Do the right thing and you shall have the power," said Emerson. Ah yes, the power! What can a person do in our world without power–the type of power that attracts other people instead of repelling them? It must be a form of power which gains momentum from the law of increasing returns, through the operation of which one's acts and deeds come back to him greatly multiplied.
The pot of gold at the end of the rainbow is not a mere fairy tale! The end of that extra mile is the spot where the rainbow ends, and that is where the pot of gold is hidden.

Few people ever arrive at the end of the rainbow. When one gets to where he thought the rainbow ended, he finds it is still far in the distance. The trouble with most of us is that we do not know how to follow rainbows. Those who know the secret know that the end of the rainbow can be reached only by going the extra mile.

The whole world is clamoring for such people. They are needed and wanted in every walk of life. American industry has always had princely berths for people who will assume responsibilities and get the job done in the right mental attitude by going the extra mile.

Andrew Carnegie lifted no fewer than forty such men from the lowly station of day laborers to millionaires. He understood the value of people who were willing to go the extra mile. Whenever he found such a person, he brought "his find" into the inner circle of his business and gave him an opportunity to earn all he was worth.

People do things or refrain from doing them because of a motive. The soundest of motives for the habit of going the extra mile is the fact that it yields enduring dividends in ways too numerous to mention, to all who follow the habit.

No one has ever been known to achieve permanent success without doing more than he was paid for. The practice has its counter-part in the laws of nature. Its soundness is backed by an impressive array of evidence. It is based on common sense and justice.

The best of all methods for testing the soundness of this principle is that of putting it to work as part of one's daily habits. Some truths we can only realize through our own experience.
We know the rules by which success is attained. Let us appropriate these rules and use them intelligently, thereby acquiring the personal riches we demand, and adding to the wealth of the nation as well.

I hope that this has been of some small benefit to you and enables you to be of greater benefit to others by going the extra mile in all you do.

Take care, take action and be relentless...

Regards,

John Millar

John Millar

Managing Director

More Profit Less Time Pty Ltd

Profit facilitator, Author, Business and Executive Coach, Trainer, Professional Speaker

Certified Business Coach, Certified NLP Practitioner, Certified Guerrilla Marketing Practitioner

Diploma of Management, Diploma of Human Resources Management, Cert IV TAE

Business Essentials Series...

Disc 1 in the Business Essentials Series
Gaining Focus in Your Business
This is about your fundamental learning skills and what you will need to do to change them to vastly improve the way you look
at your development to become a truly effective business owner not just simply remain self-employed.

You will also give you some excellent tools to set goals, work on your plans and create a diary that will allow you to steal your time back to begin moving your business from chaos to control.

Disc 2 in the Business Essentials Series
Getting Your Financials Right
You will learn the importance of understanding your financials.

After all being in business is about making profit and having cash flow work for YOU since you are responsible for your profits.
Become your accountant and book keepers best friend by understanding more about how the financials in your business works so you can ask them better questions to maximise your profits not simply ensure tax compliance.

Disc 3 in the Business Essentials Series
Leveraging Your Business Harder
You will learn the principles of what and how to leverage far more in your business to get more from less and to work far smarter and not just harder.

Here is where you will receive some of the tools you will need to better understand how to get your business flying, what it is you need to test and measure, how to do it and WHY it's so important.

Disc 4 in the Business Essentials Series
How to Generate More Clients Profitably
This is where you will determine your uniqueness, develop a meaningful guarantee and learn the basics of good advertising.

You will gain a better appreciation between the difference of Marketing and Advertising, learn how to get the most for the least investment and ensure that you do it all profitably.

Disc 5 in the Business Essentials Series
Maximising Your Conversion Rates
Get to know how your Sales Pipeline REALLY works and how to identify who your suspects really are, convert prospects into regular shoppers and understand how much more work you can do to maximise your sales experience.

Disc 6 in the Business Essentials Series

Meet and Exceed Your Clients Expectations

Now you have new customers, how do you make sure you KEEP them, how do you wanting to come back time and again while telling their friends? ...this is where you really make a difference.

Disc 7 in the Business Essentials Series

Systemising Your Business For Consistent Excellence

Do you recognise the importance of having systems in your business and how they can improve your profitability?

We show you how to systemise like a corporate while retaining the culture of a smaller business. Understanding how we systemise for routine and humanise for the exceptions will enable you to be the best in your field every time.

Disc 8 in the Business Essentials Series

Do You Have a Champion Team with a Champion Leader?

This is about having the right people on the bus. It starts with you however so you'll learn how to maximise your own skills and then you will attract and retain the right people.

When you understand how the TEAM is the most important part of your business and what needs to be done to achieve the very best from yourselves and others you are well on your way to becoming a better manager of this invaluable resource.

Disc 9 in the Business Essentials Series

The Essentials of Getting Your Time Back.

This is where you get to redefine your time management You will understand better how you can start working far more on the business than in the business than ever before.

You will also finally find out why others can seem to fit more into their day while having a great LIFE – WORK balance (notice the order!)..

Disc 10 in the Business Essentials Series

Simply Brilliant Customer Service.

It's so easy to give mediocre or good customer service but it's just as easy to give amazing service to your customers and delight them.

You will understand the simple easy steps that you must take to provide consistently brilliant service and how to get your team excited about doing it.

Disc 11 in the Business Essentials Series

Discovering DISC and EQ not just IQ.

We believe for things to change first you must change so here you will learn why you behave as you do and just as importantly understand why other people react and act the way they do.

You will also learn what DISC really is and what it isn't. You will learn how to apply these important principles in your recruitment and team management / development.

You will learn how to use these ideas in creating a more dynamic team and discover the what and why of emotional intelligence. You will also develop key strategies for using the knowledge here and the tools we have available on our website and why we place such a massive emphasis on DISC and other tools that support, train and develop your team.

You will also learn how to use these skills and observations at home and socially not just at the workplace.

Disc 12 in the Business Essentials Series
Quality Recruitment.
Recruitment of the right people for the right reasons in the right roles for your team is so incredibly important yet so often ignored or pushed to the rear.

You will learn who the right person is for your business and the role you want filled.
You will be able to identify the right people early in the process to save yourself and them the time and money wasted with antique recruitment methodologies that just don't work anymore.

How to get the best out of your recruitment activities so you can keep the assets you acquire for the long term and get the best return from your investment.

ABOUT THE AUTHOR

John Millar is the Managing Director, Senior Business Coach Trainer and Consultant with More Profit Less Time Pty Ltd and CEO-ONDEMAND. Along with his many other business interests, John is proud to have been an associate of the most successful coaching team in the world.

He is recognized as a global leader and has been benchmarked against over 1,300 colleagues in 31 countries. John has over 25 years of hands-on ownership, management, coaching, and entrepreneurial experience in a broad range of industry sectors, including retail, wholesale, import, export, IT, trades and trade services, automotive, primary production, food services, transport, manufacturing, mining, professional services, the fitness industry, and more.

He has extensive experience developing and providing training for small to medium-sized companies and a variety of publicly listed corporate companies. John is an accomplished and talented public and professional speaker. He has been a mentor working with sales/management activities for businesses with a turnover under $100,000 per annum, over $100 million turnover, and everything in between, with great success.

John currently works with business owners and their teams across Australia and has a "Whatever it takes" attitude that has enabled him to help his clients grow their business profits by up to 800%.

 If you are ready to be coached by one of the best in the business, register at:

www.ceo-ondemand.com.au

Make sure to visit www.moreprofitlesstime.com for the new online Management Development Program: The Business Essentials Series.

ACCLAIM FOR JOHN MILLAR'S
Business Coaching and Training in their own words...

"Without John Millar as my Business Coach I wouldn't have a business today."—Grant Jennings Managing Director, Jigsaw Projects

"Taking the decision to be coached and trained by John Millar was carefully considered after experiencing those who over promised and under delivered. I am pleased to say the content of his courses are the tools we all need to master as business owners. His delivery is engaging, thought provoking and empowering and after every session l came away re-energised. John always makes himself available for business building advice both via Skype and face to face beyond the scope of delivery. With his extensive personal experience in building small businesses, he knows and understands what it takes to establish and grow a business. I have no hesitation endorsing John Millar as an educator and business coach and the bonus is he is a very nice person."—Anne Lederman Managing Director FB Salons"

Johns training with my management team was excellent, it was very different from the business coaching and support I have had in the past. John was clear, thoughtful and he addressed the issues we needed to cover without us even knowing they were being addressed! His follow up has been fantastic and exactly what I needed. I would recommend John and his team to anyone looking at getting some business coaching and training done" —Wendy Crawford, Peopleworx

"In my dealings with John as our business coach, I have found him to be a motivated and insightful agent of positive change. He is able to burrow down to the root cause of issues and introduce effective forms of measurement. John then identifies and implements practical solutions and is there to provide the gentle persuasion required to ensure that results are achieved." —Mark Felton, Lindale Insurances

"You have coached and trained us so well throughout the year that we are now used to & find it easy to prepare a 90 day plan, then breaks it down to actionable bite size pieces. Planning in business & personal life certainly is important. It allows us to identify the important things & the bigger picture. Thank you for your support & guidance throughout the year. And not to mention your insight, external perspective to review & assist our business moving forward." —Linda Turner, Director Roy A McDonald Certified Practicing Accountants

"If you want to achieve sales results you never thought were possible and give yourself a competitive edge my strong suggestion is to engage John services and listen closely to what John has to say, during the time I was trained by John I was one of eight sales consultants in a national business for 10 out of the 13 months I lead the sales tally and in 1 quarter I generated three times the revenue of the national sales force combined. Johns training and experience was well worth the investment and paid big dividends. Thanks John." —Julian Fadini, Bellvue Capital

"John is a very enthusiastic trainer and business coach, he is very passionate about getting business owners and their team where they need to be. He goes the extra mile to keep ahead of the latest developments which he then uses to benefit his clients." —Darren Reddy CPA

"I have been to a few seminars and heard John speak numerous times about sales, marketing and business. He is a very knowledgeable and extremely enthusiastic business coach in all his interactions and I would recommend him to all business owners who need a sales and marketing boost!" —Andrew Heath, Managing Director, Fresh Living Group

"I worked with John Millar and found his business knowledge, passion and innovation to be inspiring. He has always been able to set (and achieve) strategic long and short-term goals both for himself and his clients without losing that personal connection he builds with everyone he meets. He has been and I believe will continue to be a strong mentor and trainer for anyone wanting to take that next step in their business." —Bree Webster, Online Marketing Guru

"Massive Action Day" – what an understatement, John Millars 4 hour frenzy challenged me to seriously review areas of my business I would not have gone to …. In this way, the process identified incongruence's in my mind, my business and my modus operandi. It's created a paradigm shift. Thanks John, the road map just got a whole lot clearer. Your friendship and insights since 2003 have been a gift to my business and I." —Andrew Reay, Counsellor, Hypnotherapist and Counsellor, Thinkshift Transformations

"John Millar is not your usual Business coach or trainer; he gets involved with you and your business and provides hands on help to make sure you follow through on his advice. He is highly motivated to help his clients and his personal guarantee certainly shows this. He has now transposed his thoughts, advice and love of good business onto a series of DVD's in his business venture – More Profit Less Time. This has excellent tips and advice for anyone either starting out or already in business. I highly recommend John to any business owner who wants to run a business and not a j.o.b.!" —Darren Cassidy, Managing Director HR2U

"I and many of my Business Partners and colleagues have worked with John since 2010 as our business oath, trainer and motivator and found him to be an extremely motivational person to assist us achieve our business goals. This company and its products allows for John's skill set to be accessed by a wider number of potential clients. His very professional DVD series is extremely good value for money and is easily accessible for all of us who are time poor. If you are looking to maximise your and your business's results and to start achieving your goals and dreams, contact John; you won't look back!!" —Mark Cleland, Mortgage Choice

"John develops real relationships with the people he comes into contact with. He is pasionate about what he does. His DVD and group training series, is full of good ideas and process to make your business better. Knowing what to do and actually doing it are two different things. John is excellent at helping you get things done." —Carey Rudd, Sales Director, Online Knowledge

"I have known John since 2004 and found him to be extremely knowledgably in both Sales and Business systems as a business coach without peer. John has provided me with business advice as well as personal coaching over the years, helping me with the running of my organisation. I'm impressed with John's DVD series where he has condensed a lot of the information in an easy to follow format that any business owner can use immediately. I wish he had released these DVDs earlier, as they are a goldmine of information, and practical how to that allow anyone to increase the profit in their business and get back valuable wasted time." —Steve Psaradellis, Managing Director, TEBA

"John's DVD and workbook delivery of his no-nonsense advice provides a low-cost option for those business owners looking to set and achieve goals that will increase profit. I found the conversational style of the DVD's easy to follow, whilst the requirement to pause the DVD and write down some action points ensured a level of commitment to the advice being provided." — Mark Felton, Lindale Insurances

"I only met John briefly at a BNI meeting and knew instantly i need to hire him for my business as my business coach. His attitude towards work and how to improve my cash line had an instant effect on before, even before I finally hired him on an official basis. I found myself thinking "what would John do" and this was only after just meeting him. I cannot see my business expend and give me "More Profit Less Time" without John's expert direction and training. If you want to succeed in business life, you need John Millar, without him you're just kidding yourself " —Leslie Cachia, Managing Director, Letac Drafting

"I can highly recommend John Millar to any business owner who wants to grow his business. When I hear very positive feedback from colleagues who are skeptics by nature about John's ability and skills, I know John will help all those he comes in contact with. John comes with a selfless nature and the willingness to work inside a client's business to make it succeed. Rare indeed!" —Darren Cassidy, Managing Director, HR2U"I first met John Millar in mid-2010 and have always found him to be of an honest and generous character that engenders an easy association with him. I love how easy he is to listen to and how passionate he is about his work and topics. John demonstrates a love for life and his work and I have no hesitation in recommending his services." —Kathie M Thomas, Managing Director, VA

"I have listened to John speak on a number of occasions and find him a very knowledgeable speaker with a passion for what he does. I have also interacted with a number of his clients and they all tell me that he helps them achieve results in their business. If you are looking for business help John is a person you can trust." —Carey Rudd, Sales Director, Online Knowledge

"John knows his stuff, he knows how the get results, John has so many great ideas in building a business and helping business owners work less and make more money. John has released a DVD set on doing just that. I have watched the 1st one and it was great, very informative and easy to understand, I happily recommend John to anyone in need of help and guidance" —Frank Eramo, Proprietor, Dynotune

"I have known John only for a short time, however the impact that he has had on me, not just my business has helped me to visualise opportunities that I began to doubt my ability to realise. He is encouraging and at the same time challenging so that he can/you can, begin to see how to maximise the business potential, John calls it being an unreasonable friend, I call it being a mate. If you have any questions about the direction of your business, if you want to seem your bottom line improve not just turnover but real profit, if you want a person who will work with you then I strongly recommend that you engage him at your earliest convenience. John is the best thing that has happened to my business. I could tell you about the way he is on track to make 1/2 a million for me on his contacts alone, but that actually sells him short, he has become like my partner in business, and cares about my success as if it was his own, we will flourish because I took the step to employ his training to help me grow. If you get a chance to get him training you, don't wait like I did, get in as quickly as possible, his time is your business and if like me your business is to make money, then every day you don't have him on retainer you lose money." —Russell Summers, Managing Director, The Give Life Centre

"It's usually easy to be mediocre in business but it's impossible when you have John Millar training you. He has been my right hand since 2003!" —David Manser, CFO, Hydrosteer

"I now have a commercial, profitable business and now it's my choice when I work IN my business and when I work ON it and have had john helping me in business since 1988. I can't imagine not having John as a part of our business." —David Wall, Director, D&K Transport

"The work John has done since 2008 coaching and training our marketing team, administration and finance teams, buyers, store managers and staff nationally have been fantastic." —Ross Sudano, Director, Anaconda Adventure Stores

"John is a creative, professional, practical and committed business coach and trainer. His approach since we first met him in 1994 to working with a client team through the application of useful tools, information and anecdotes along with his easy going & easy to understand delivery sets him apart from other business coaches that I have used in the past." —Anthony Beasley, Director, The Astra Group

"I have worked with John Millar for the since 2004 and I didn't think it was possible to achieve what we have achieved together. His business coaching, training and services just get better and better!" —Terrance Chong, Managing Director, Echo Graphics and Printing

"John's business coaching, training and support has transformed our business across Australia and New Zealand since 2008."—Rose Vis, Managing Director, VIP Australia

"We first met John in 2005, he is AMAZING at sales, marketing, operations, logistics, finance training and so much more. Since engaging John as our business coach our business has exploded, our team are happy, our clients are raving about us and my husband and I now take at least 12 weeks holidays a year, EVERY year." —Shirley Du, Director, Goldline Technology

"It's the no nonsense results driven business coaching and training focus John bought to the table that had such a massive effect on our business." —David Runkel, Director, Tracomp Fabrication and Steel

"We started working with John in early 2010, within 90 days of working with and being trained by John Millar we had the biggest and most profitable month in our 15 year history. That's impressive." —Hugh Gilchrist, Managing Director, Australian Moulding Company

"If you don't have John as your business trainer you aren't meeting your business potential." —Don Robertson, Director, Medallion Electrical Services

Thank You